When Rosie O'Donnell first asked kids to send her their best jokes, thousands of young viewers all across the country immediately flooded her mailbox with drawings, letters, and of course, great puns and riddles. Soon Rosie was sharing the funniest jokes and pictures with her audience . . . and a much loved feature on "The Rosie O'Donnell Show" was born. Here are some of Rosie's favorites—all guaranteed to bring smiles and laughter into your day.

All profits from this book go to the For All Kids Foundation, P.O. Box 225, Allendale, NJ 07401, which is devoted to children's charities.

Dania Gold, age 7½

Shayley Rae Wright, age 7

Jokes Sent by Kids to
The Rosie O'Donnell Show

WARNER BOOKS

A Time Warner Company

Warner Books, Inc., 1271 Avenue of the Americas, New York, NY 10020
W A Time Warner Company

Printed in the United States of America

First Trade Paperback Printing: June 1997

10 9 8 7 6 5 4 3 2 1

ISBN: 0-446-22218-6

Text design by Stanley S. Drate/Folio Graphics Co. Inc.
Front cover photo by Janette Beckman
Back cover photo by Joe Viles © Warner Bros.

Introduction
by Rosie O'Donnell

I remember the first joke I ever heard.

    Q. "Why did the boy throw the clock
       out the window?"

    A. "He wanted to see time fly."

Not very funny, I know.

    Billy Sheerin was the kid who knew all the jokes. We were both in third grade at Rolling Hills Elementary School, Commack, Long Island. Miss Boy was our teacher, and a great one at that. She read to us every day, encouraged us to be creative, to write, to draw, to paint. I was kinda shy back then, sitting quietly in the last row, wishing I could be a little more like Billy Sheerin.

    Billy was fearless. I think he knew every joke there was, and wasn't afraid to tell them. When he ran out, he made some up. Silly, nonsensical jokes . . .

    Q. "Why is the rug green?"

    A. " 'Cause my sneakers are blue."

    Then he would roar with laughter. Contagious, side-splitting, milk-coming-out-of-your-nose-type laughter. Before long, the whole class was laughing with him. I can still see his shaggy blond hair, sparkly blue eyes, and loopy grin. To me, Billy Sheerin was the king.

Thanks to all the kids who wrote in. To the moms and dads who addressed the envelopes.

Thanks to the kindhearted people at Warner Books.

All profits from this book go to charity.

I hope this is only the beginning.

MONSTROSITIES

What do sea monsters eat for lunch?

Fish and ships.

✦

Who belongs to the monster PTA?

Mummies and Deadies.

✦

What do you say when you cross a two-headed monster?

Hello, hello, goodbye, goodbye!

✦

Who is a monster's favorite comedian?

Blob Newhart.

✦

Who is a monster's favorite comedienne?

Hairy Tyler Moore.

Where is a monster's favorite place to swim?

Lake Eerie.

◆

What happened when the monster ate the electric company?

He was in shock for a week.

◆

Why did the sea monster eat five ships that were carrying potatoes?

No one can eat just one potato ship.

---◆---

BOO WHO?

What does a ghost call his mother and father?

His trans-parents.

◆

Why did Dewie give the ghost a bandage?

It had a boo-boo.

What does a ghost eat for breakfast?

Scream of wheat.

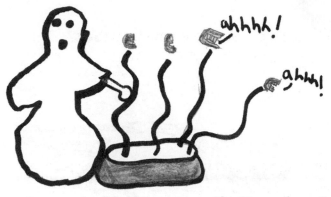

ahhhh!

ahhh!

Alan Maynard, age 8

What do ghosts eat for lunch?

Booghetti and meatballs.

What kind of candy do ghosts like to eat?

Booble gum.

What patriotic song do ghosts like best?

"America the Boo-tiful."

Where do ghosts put their mail?

In the ghost office!

◆

What do ghosts wear when it snows?

Booooots.

Taylor Fries, age 7

What is a ghost's favorite TV shows?

"*The Broody Bunch*" *and* "*Ghouligan's Island.*"

✦

What happens when a banana sees a ghost?

The banana splits.

✦

Who did Frankenstein bring to the Valentine's Day dance?

His ghoul-friend.

Sam Frizell

What does a mother ghost say to her children when they get into the car?

Fasten your sheet belts.

WITCHES, DEVILS AND OTHER WORLDLY FRIENDS

Lola Dalrymple, age 7

What do you call two witches who live together?

Broom-mates.

◆

How do you make a witch scratch?

Take away her **w**.

Aimee Rachele Zisner, age 9

Why did the witches call off the baseball game?

They couldn't find the bats.

❖

What do you get when you put a Tasmanian devil into a chicken coop?

Deviled eggs.

what is
mummys
favorite
kind of music

wrap music

Ryan Heaney

Why did the cyclops have to shut down his school?

He had only one pupil.

✦

Why didn't the skeleton cross the road?

He didn't have the guts.

✦

How do you make a skeleton laugh?

By tickling his funny bone.

✦

What is a skeleton afraid of?

A dog, because it likes bones.

✦

Why don't skeletons play music in church?

Because they don't have any guts.

What's the vampire's favorite holiday?

Fangsgiving.

◆

Why doesn't anybody kiss a vampire?

Because he has bat breath.

◆

Why is the Jolly Green Giant a good gardener?

He has two green thumbs.

---◆---

ANIMALS, ANIMALS

What's Your Beef?

How do you count cows?

With a cowculator.

What famous beach do cows go to for the holidays?

Moooami Beach.

◆

What is a cow's favorite TV show?

"Steer Trek."

◆

Why did the farmer buy a brown cow?

Because he wanted chocolate milk.

◆

What do you call a cow that eats grass?

A lawn moooer.

◆

Where can you find the most cows?

Moo York.

◆

Where do cows go on a Saturday night?

To the mooovies.

What do you call a cow with no legs?

Ground beef.

✦

What do you call a cow that doesn't give milk?

A milk dud.

✦

What do you get when you cross a cow with a duck?

Milk and quackers.

✦

Where does the cow artist put his paintings?

In the moooseum.

✦

What do you get from a nervous cow?

A milk shake.

Which class do cows like?

Mooosic class.

✦

Where do steers go to dance?

The meat ball.

✦

What do you call a bull that's sleeping?

A bulldozer.

✦

What TV show is about investigating mysterious cattle?

"The Ox-Files."

Amazing Dog Tails

What is more amazing than a talking dog?

A spelling bee.

✦

How does a dog stop a VCR?

He presses the paws button.

What would you call a cold puppy sitting on a rabbit?

A chili dog on a bun.

◆

What do you get when you cross a dog with a hen?

Pooched eggs.

◆

What's the difference between a dog and a painter?

One sheds his coat and the other coats his shed.

◆

What's Lassie's favorite vegetable?

Collie-flower.

Daria Kaliman

What did the dog say when he sat on sandpaper?

Rough! Rough!

✦

Where should you never take a dog?

To the flea market.

✦

What do you call a three-legged dog?

Skippy.

✦

Why did the Dalmatian go to the cleaner's?

His coat had spots all over it.

✦

What has a coat all winter and pants in the summer?

A dog.

✦

Why did the man bring his dog to the railroad station?

To train him.

What dog keeps the best time?

A watchdog.

Cat Tails Too

What do cats eat for breakfast?

Mice Krispies.

Taylor and Donald Fries,
ages 7 & 11

What does an invisible cat drink?

Evaporated milk.

◆

What do cats cook when they're in a hurry?

Minute-mice.

What do you call a cat that falls into a trash can?

Kitty litter.

✦

Where does a cat go when he loses his tail?

To a retail store.

✦

If ten cats were in a boat and one jumped out, how many would be left in the boat?

None, they were all copycats.

✦

How do you spell *mouse traps* using three letters.

C-A-T.

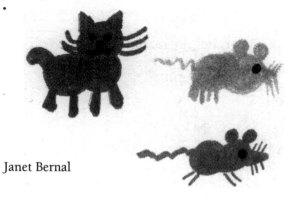

Janet Bernal

What animal should you never play cards with?

A cheetah.

✦

Why can't cheetahs hide very well?

Because they are always spotted.

✦

Why did the lion spit out the clown?

Because he tasted funny.

Babe Jokes

What do you get when you cross a karate expert with a pig?

A porkchop.

✦

What do pigs do after school?

Their hamwork.

What kind of medicine does a pig take?

Oinkment.

◆

Why did the farmer name his pig "Ink"?

Because it kept running out of the pen.

More Animals

What do you call 100 rabbits jumping backward?

A receding hare line.

◆

Where do rabbits go after they get married?

On a bunnymoon.

◆

What is a squirrel's favorite ballet?

"The Nut Cracker."

What do you get when you cross a rabbit with a spider?

A hare net.

Christie Falco, age 8

How do you catch a squirrel?

Climb up a tree and act like a nut.

◆

What kind of pine is the sharpest?

A porcupine.

Adele Hetrick

Why did the hyena bang his head on the piano keys?

He was playing by ear.

◆

What kind of key does not unlock any door?

A monkey.

◆

How did the rodeo horse get so rich?

He had a lot of bucks.

Why couldn't the pony talk?

He was a little horse.

✦

Why do mother kangaroos hate rainy days?

Because their kids have to play inside.

✦

What mouse won't eat cheese?

A computer mouse.

✦

What happened to the mouse that fell off the shelf and into a glass of Mountain Dew?

Nothing, it was a soft drink.

✦

Why did the turtle cross the road?

To get to the shell station.

✦

Where does the lamb get his hair cut?

The baaaaber.

What do you call a shy lamb?

Baaaashful.

✦

When are sheep like ink?

When they are in a pen.

✦

What animal can you put in the washing machine?

A wash-and-werewolf.

✦

What kind of animal can jump higher than the Empire State Building?

Any animal—the Empire State Building can't jump!

✦

What does a moose get when he lifts weights?

Moosles.

Why do giraffes have long necks?

Because their feet stink!

✦

How do you keep a rhinoceros from charging?

Take away its credit cards.

✦

Why did the bear tiptoe through the campground?

He didn't want to wake up the sleeping bags.

✦

How many paws does a bear have?

One paw and one maw.

✦

What does a polar bear telephone operator say?

Glad I could help you. Have an ice day.

What did the teddy bear say when he was offered dessert?

No thanks, I'm stuffed.

Alicia Best, age 8

What are Dino bandages for?

Dinosores.

Amanda Tellier, age 7

What do you call a scared tyrannosaurus?

A nervous rex.

◆

What do you get when two dinosaurs crash?

A tyrannosaurus wreck.

Feathered Friends

Why do ducks fly south?

Because it's too far to walk.

QUACK!
QUACK!

Sarah Ford

Laura Victor, age 4

Why didn't the duck eat his soup?

He couldn't find his quackers.

◆

What goes *kcauq, kcauq?*

A duck flying backward.

◆

If chickens get up when the rooster crows, when do ducks get up?

At the quack of dawn.

What day do chickens hate the most?

Fry-day.

✦

Why didn't the rooster cross the road?

Because he was too chicken.

✦

Why did the chicken cross the playground?

To get to the other slide.

✦

Why did the chicken lay an egg?

Because if she dropped it, it would break.

John Aherne

Where did the chicken go on her vacation?

Sandy Eggo.

✦

Why don't seagulls hang out at the bay?

Then they'd be bagels.

✦

What do birds love for dessert?

Dove bars.

✦

Whom do birds love?

Their tweet hearts.

✦

What do you get when you cross a parrot with a centipede?

A walkie-talkie.

✦

How did the parrot get to the vet?

He flu.

What do you call an owl with a sore throat?

A bird that doesn't give a hoot.

Bees and Fleas and Other Things that Bug Us

What did the mother bee say to the naughty baby bee?

Beehive yourself.

Ben, Dan and David Moulton, ages 5, 9, and 11

Why do bees hum?

Because they don't know the words.

David Schlesinger

How can you tell if a bee is on the phone?

You get a busy signal.

Why do bees itch?

Because they have hives.

What is a bee's favorite soap opera?

"Days of Our Hives."

What did the flea say to the other flea?

Should we walk or take a dog?

Why is the father centipede so upset?

All the kids need new shoes.

What did the mother lightning bug say to the father lightning bug?

Junior sure is bright.

✦

What happened to the two bedbugs who fell in love?

They got married in the spring.

✦

Where do you find the world's biggest spider?

In the World Wide Web.

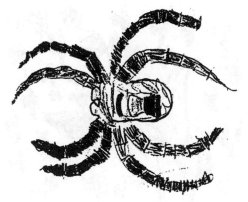

Emma and Ben Ilaria, ages 6 and 2½

Billy Yates, age 7

Something's Fishy

Where is the best place to see a man-eating fish?

A seafood restaurant.

Adam Schlesinger

Why do fish have such huge phone bills?

Because when they get on the line they can't get off.

✦

How do you communicate with a fish?

Drop him a line.

✦

Why don't fish go near computers?

They're afraid of getting caught in the Internet.

✦

What do you call a fish with two legs?

A two-knee fish.

✦

What did the shrimp yell when he got caught in the seaweed?

Kelp! Kelp!!

Why is it so easy to weigh a fish?

It comes with scales.

◆

Why are fish so smart?

Because they swim in schools.

Melanie Jacobs

Why wouldn't the oyster give anyone his pearl?

He was shellfish.

◆

What is a fish's favorite game show?

"Name that Tuna."

◆

What did the boy octopus say to the girl octopus?

I want to hold your hand, hand, hand, hand . . .

A Few Stinky Jokes

What do you call a skunk in court?

Odor in the court.

✦

What are the most commonly used letters in the skunk alphabet?

P and U.

✦

How did the skunk call home?

On his smellular phone.

✦

How many skunks does it take to stink up a room?

A phew.

And Some Really Slimy Jokes

What did the snake give his girlfriend on their first date?

A goodnight hiss.

Why do you measure snakes in inches?

Because they have no feet.

◆

If a snake and an undertaker got married, what would their towels say?

Hiss and Hearse.

◆

What's worse than finding a worm in your apple?

Finding half a worm.

Melissa Ross, age 7

What does a worm do in a cornfield?

He goes in one ear and out the other.

What does a cobra learn in college?

Hisssstory.

◆

What do you get when you stack toads together?

A toadempole.

◆

What year do frogs like best?

Leap year!

◆

What happens when a frog is parked illegally?

It's toad away.

◆

What does a frog drink when he's on a diet?

Diet Croak.

QUESTIONABLE CHARACTERS

What are Batman and Robin called after they get run over by a bus?

Flatman and Robin.

◆

Why do airplane pilots always fly past Peter Pan's home?

They see the sign "Never Never Land."

◆

What did Snow White say when she was waiting for her photos?

Someday my prints will come.

◆

Why did the baseball coach throw Cinderella off the team?

Because she ran away from the ball.

Why did Little Bo-Peep put chocolate sauce on her sheep?

Because she wanted a candy baaaaaaaaaah.

◆

What is Santa's favorite kind of sandwich?

Peanut butter and jolly.

◆

Where did Santa go on his vacation?

To a ho-ho hotel.

◆

How does Ebenezer Scrooge make phone calls?

Collect.

◆

Why did Mickey Mouse go up to outer space?

To find Pluto.

◆

What kind of car does Luke Skywalker drive?

A Toy Yoda.

What is Tarzan's favorite song?

"Jungle Bells."

✦

What did Ernie say when Bert asked him if he wanted ice cream?

Sure, Bert.

✦

What's red, furry, and knocks you over?

Tackle-Me Elmo.

✦

What do you call a fairy who has not taken a bath in a week?

Stinkerbell.

✦

HISTORY QUIZ

What do George Washington, Abraham Lincoln, and Christopher Columbus have in common?

They were all born on a holiday.

Where was the Declaration of Independence signed?

At the bottom.

✦

If April showers bring May flowers, then what do May flowers bring?

Pilgrims.

✦

Why was George Washington buried standing up?

Because he never lied.

✦

What's black and white, black and white, black and white?

A penguin rolling down a hill.

✦

What's black and white and red all over?

A zebra with a sunburn.

✦

Why do you need to take a baseball player with you when you go camping?

To pitch the tent.

✦

Why did the cop run across the baseball field?

Someone stole second base.

✦

Why is a cake like a baseball team?

They both need a good batter.

✦

Why are spiders good baseball players?

Because they are good at catching flies.

✦

Where did the baseball player wash his socks?

In the bleachers.

Why was the Orioles' stadium so hot after the game?

All the fans had left.

◆

Does it take longer to run from first base to second, or from second to third?

From second to third, because there is a shortstop in the middle.

◆

Where is the largest diamond in New York City kept?

In Yankee Stadium.

◆

Why were the players wearing armor at the ballpark?

It was a knight game.

◆

Where does a catcher sit for dinner?

Behind the plate.

Which sports player is the sloppiest eater?

A basketball player, because he dribbles all over.

◆

Why aren't the Vancouver Grizzlies hot?

Because they have a lot of fans.

Gustavo Benzan

When is a basketball player like a baby?

When he dribbles.

◆

Why did the basketball player throw the basketball in the water?

Because his coach told him to sink it.

What did the basketball player ask for from the genie?

Three swishes.

◆

How does a hockey player kiss?

He puckers up.

◆

What do you give a hockey player when he demands money?

A check.

◆

What position did the monster play on the soccer team?

Ghoulie.

◆

Why do soccer players have so much trouble eating popcorn balls?

They think they can't use their hands.

What did the bowling ball say to the bowling pins?

Don't stop me, I'm on a roll!

✦

Why does a football player always carry a spare pencil?

In case he needs an extra point.

✦

Why did the football coach go to the bank?

To get his quarterback.

✦

Why did the golfer wear two pairs of pants?

In case he got a hole in one.

✦

When is the best time to long-jump?

In a leap year.

If athletes get athlete's foot, what do astronauts get?

Missile-toe.

FOOD FOR THOUGHT

What is a potato's favorite TV show?

"Mash."

What kind of fruit do you feed a scarecrow?

Strawberries.

Why were all the baby strawberries crying?

Because their mommy was in a jam.

How do you fix a broken pizza?

With tomato paste.

If I had six oranges in one hand and seven in the other, what would I have?

Very big hands.

Adam Schlesinger

What did the grape say when he got squished?

Nothing, he just let out a little wine.

◆

What do you call two banana peels?

A pair of slippers.

◆

What is the father of all corn?

Pop*corn.*

Why did the tomato turn red?

He saw the salad dressing.

◆

Why did the cookie go to the hospital?

Because he was feeling crummy.

Natasha Parker, age 12

Why did the orange stop?

Because he ran out of juice.

◆

What kind of food is crazy about money?

A doughnut.

Why couldn't the egg lend money to the troll?

It was broke.

✦

Why did the radish kiss the banana?

Because it had appeal.

✦

What kind of apple isn't an apple?

A pineapple.

✦

A peanut sat on a railroad track.
His heart was all a-flutter.
The five-fifteen came rushing by.
"Toot! Toot!" Peanut butter!

✦

Why did the watermelons have to have a formal wedding?

Cant-elope.

Why did the orange go to the doctor?

He wasn't peeling well.

Ben Cole, age 8

What kind of cheese comes with a house?

Cottage cheese.

✦

What's the laziest vegetable?

A couch potato.

Meagan Moran, age 9

What did one sandwich say to the other?

Boy, you're full of bologna.

◆

What did the mayonnaise say to the refrigerator door?

Shut the door, I'm dressing!

◆

Why does steak taste better in space?

Because it's meteor.

If a carrot and a cabbage ran a race, who would win?

The cabbage would, because it's a head.

✦

What did the banana bandits say when they got caught?

Let's split!

✦

Did you hear about the big fight at the candy store last night?

Two suckers got licked.

✦

What kind of candy do kids eat on the playground?

Recess Pieces.

✦

Why didn't the hot dog star in the movies?

Because the rolls weren't good enough.

How do you make a hamburger roll?

Take it to a hill and give it a push.

◆

What did one plate say to the other plate?

Lunch is on me.

◆

Did you hear about the new restaurant on the moon?

Great food, but no atmosphere.

Alyssa B. Figueroa, age 9

NATURE CALLS

Why isn't it safe to tell a secret in a garden?

Because the corn have ears and the beanstalk.

◆

Why does the ocean roar?

You would too if you had crabs in your bed!

◆

What did the ocean say to the beach?

Nothing, it just waved.

Kawena H. Matsumoto

Why are flowers so lazy?

Because they always stay in bed.

◆

What did the dirt say when it began to rain?

If this keeps up, my name will be mud.

◆

What falls in the winter and never gets hurt?

Snow.

◆

What's faster, heat or cold?

Heat—you can catch a cold.

◆

What does the sun drink out of?

Sunglasses.

◆

How is the sun like a black eye?

Both are shiners.

What is the difference between one yard and two yards?

Usually a fence.

Why don't 5 and 6 like 7?

Because 7, 8, 9.

If 2 is company and 3 is a crowd, what are 4 and 5?

9.

What did one math book say to the other?

I really have a lot of problems.

What happened to the plant on the windowsill of the math classroom?

It grew square roots.

How many jelly beans can you put in an empty jar?

Only one—after that, the jar isn't empty anymore.

Rosie,
How much does it cost a pirate to get his ears pirced?

A buckkan-ear!

Katy and Sean Henry

What has 100 legs but cannot walk?

Fifty pairs of pants.

How do you make gold soup?

Add fourteen karats.

✦

Is a hammer a useful tool in math class?

No, but multi-pliers are.

---✦---

FUNNY BONES AND OTHER BODY PARTS

What do you do when your nose goes on strike?

You pick it!

✦

What did one eye say to the other eye?

Between you and me, something smells.

✦

What flowers grow between your nose and your chin?

Tulips.

Why did the heart get kicked off the band?

It skipped a beat.

◆

What evidence do you have that you were built upside down?

Your nose runs and your feet smell.

◆

What did one hair say to the other hair?

It takes two to tangle.

————————— ◆ —————————

MOVING ON

Why did the car stop in the middle of the road?

Because it was wheely, wheely tired.

◆

When is a car not a car?

When it turns into a driveway.

When is a car door not a car door?

When it's ajar.

✦

What has wheels and flies?

A garbage truck.

✦

What do you get when you cross a broom with a motorcycle?

A broom-broom broomstick.

✦

What do you call a freight train loaded with bubble gum?

A chew-chew train.

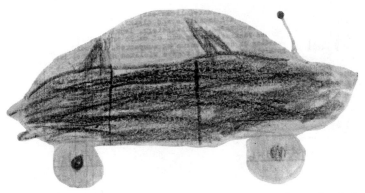

Jesse Cardiel

DUMB-PEOPLE JOKES

Why did grandma knit three socks for her grandson?

Because he grew a foot.

◆

Why did the girl throw the butter outside?

She wanted to see the butterfly.

◆

Why did the lady put lipstick on her head?

Because she wanted to make-up her mind.

◆

What is Beethoven doing in his grave?

Decomposing.

If you are an American outside of the bathroom, what are you in the bathroom?

European.

◆

What do you call a boy with a dictionary in his pocket?

Smarty Pants.

Lauren Young, age 5

What does a baker put on his bed?

Cookie sheets.

◆

Why did the scientist install a knocker on his door?

He wanted to win the No-Bell Prize.

◆

Why was the scientist's head wet?

Because he had a brainstorm.

Jasmine Jacob, age 6

What kind of gum does a scientist chew?

Ex-speariment.

✦

Why didn't the astronaut go to class?

It was launch time.

✦

Who made the first airplane that could not fly?

The Wrong Brothers.

✦

What does a farmer give his wife on Valentine's Day?

Hogs and kisses.

✦

How did the farmer mend his pants?

With cabbage patches.

✦

Why should you never marry a tennis player?

Because love means nothing to them.

What do you call a grouchy person at the beach?

A sandcrab.

✦

Where do cowboys cook their breakfast?

On the range.

✦

What did the cowboy say to the pencil?

Draw, partner.

✦

Why does a cowboy ride a horse?

Because it's too heavy to carry.

✦

Three men were standing under one umbrella, but no one got wet. How can this be?

It wasn't raining.

✦

A man went to the rocket station and asked for a ticket to the moon.

"Sorry, sir," said the attendant, "the moon is full just now."

What is the difference between a teacher and a train?

A teacher says "Spit out your gum" and a train says "Chew chew."

◆

ERIKA: Ms. Johnson, would you get mad at me for something I didn't do?
MS. JOHNSON: Of course not, Erika.
ERIKA: Good. Because I didn't do my homework!

◆

Why did the boy stick a hose in his friend's ear?

He was trying to brainwash him.

Terrance Mooney, age 7

Why did the kids wear bathing suits to school?

They rode in a carpool.

◆

Why did the kid put his dad in the refrigerator?

Because he wanted a cold pop.

◆

Why did the girl go outside with her purse open?

She wanted to see if there was any change in the weather.

◆

Why did the man put sugar in his pillow?

He wanted to have sweet dreams.

◆

What's Irish and sits outside in the summer?

Patio furniture.

◆

Why did the woman wear a helmet at the dinner table?

She was on a crash diet.

Why do some fishermen use helicopters to catch their morning bait?

Because the whirly-bird catches the worms.

✦

A dad went into a pet store and asked the owner if he could have a cat for his son.

The owner said, "Sorry, we don't do trades."

✦

Why did the man wear a rabbit as a hat?

Because he didn't want anyone to harm a hare on his head.

✦

Why did the little girl take a candy bar to her dentist appointment?

She wanted a chocolate filling.

✦

Why did the man pour veggies all over the world?

He wanted peas on Earth.

Did you hear about the man who stayed up all night trying to find out where the sun went?

It finally dawned on him.

Sara Tillotson

Where did the inventor of the toupee get his idea?

Off the top of his head.

◆

What do police officers buy at the bakery?

Copcakes.

What actress really takes the cake?

Doris Daynish!

Adam Quick, age 6

Why couldn't the pirate play cards?

He was sitting on the deck.

---◆---

KNOCK-KNOCK

Knock-knock.
Who's there?
Dwayne.
Dwayne who?
Dwayne the bathtub, I'm dwowning!

Knock-knock.
Who's there?
Boo.
Boo who?
You don't have to cry, it's just a joke.

✦

Knock-knock.
Who's there?
Little old lady.
Little old lady who?
I didn't know you could yodel.

✦

Knock-knock.
Who's there?
Ben.
Ben who?
Ben knocking on the door all afternoon.

✦

Knock-knock.
Who's there?
Roach.
Roach who?
Roach you a letter—did you get it?

Knock-knock.
Who's there?
Wanda witch.
Wanda witch who?
Wanda witch you a Happy Valentine's Day.

Knock-knock.
Who's there?
Etch.
Etch who?
Bless you!

Knock-knock.
Who's there?
Cows go.
Cows go who?
Cows don't go who, they go moo.

What word starts with *e*, ends with *e*, and only has one letter in it?

Envelope.

If all the letters were invited to a tea party, what letters would be late?

*The letters **U**, **V**, **W**, **X**, **Y**, and **Z**. They all come after **T**.*

Brittny Alcover

SILLY QUESTIONS, SMART ANSWERS

How do you make a tissue dance?

Put a little boogie in it.

Francesca and Diana Brescia, ages 9 and 8

What's the easiest way to get on TV?

Sit on it.

How do you say "chocolate" in French?

Chocolate in French.

✦

Why don't you iron a four-leaf clover?

You might press your luck.

✦

What goes up when the rain comes down?

An umbrella.

✦

What is easy to get into but hard to get out of?

Trouble.

✦

Where's King Solomon's Temple?

On the other side of his head.

✦

Why did the bubble gum cross the road?

Because it was stuck to the chicken's foot.

Why is a cookbook exciting?

It has many stirring events.

✦

What do you call a boomerang that doesn't come back?

A stick.

✦

How do you make a bandstand?

Take away their chairs.

✦

Which will burn longer, the birthday candles of a boy or the birthday candles of a girl?

No candles burn longer—they all burn shorter.

Taylor Watson

Why did the candle fall in love?

He met the perfect match.

◆

What did one candle say to another?

Are you going out tonight?

Jesse Cardiel

How do angels answer the phone?

Halo.

◆

What do you do if you're trapped in a candy store with a bomb?

Grab a Life Saver.

What do space aliens eat for breakfast?

Flying sausages.

✦

What is the tallest building in your city?

The library—it has the most stories.

✦

What did one library book say to the other?

Can I take you out?

✦

Why do clocks seem so shy?

Because they always have their hands in front of their faces!

✦

What did the knife say to the other knife?

You're looking sharp today!

✦

What did the cuffs say to the collar?

Sleeve us alone.

What did the necktie say to the hat?

   You go ahead, I'll just hang around.

◆

What did the paper clip say to the magnet?

   I find you attractive.

◆

What did one gas tank say to the other gas tank?

   What do you take me for, a fuel?

◆

What do you do when your smoke alarm goes off?

   Run after it.

◆

What do you get when you drop a piano down the mine shaft?

   A flat miner.

Why did the light turn red?

Wouldn't you turn red if you were caught changing in the middle of the street?

What company has the cutest ships going to the Bahamas?

Tanya Alvear, age 9

Tom Cruise Lines

What is the state you can wear?

New Jersey.

What room can a student never enter?

A mushroom.

✦

What kind of dress do you have that you never wear?

Your address.

✦

How can you tell a toy is nervous?

It's all wound up.

✦

How did the piano get out of jail?

With its keys.

✦

ROSIE JOKES

What happens when you cross Rosie with a Ring Ding?

Ring around Rosie.

Christopher Stelman, age 5

What do you get when you cross a flower with a ship?

A Rosie cruise.

◆

What does Rosie O'Donnell's doorbell say?

Ring-ding, ring-ding.

◆

What did Nicole Kidman say to Rosie O'Donnell?

You're cruisin' for a bruisin'.

Did you hear what happened when Rosie and Tom tried to kiss in the fog?

They mist!

Juanita Gabaldon

Rosie

Knock-knock.
Who's there?
Olive.
Olive who?
Olive ya, Rosie.

Becky Hoffman,
age 12

My Special Thanks
to All the Children Who Sent in Their Wonderful Jokes and Pictures!

◆

A.J.	Autumn	Carrie	Diana
Adam	Bailey	Carrie Anne	Donald
Adele	Becky	Charlie	Douglas
Andrew	Ben	Chelsea	Dustin
Alan	Bethany	Chelsi	Dylan
Alana	Billy	Cheta	Eleanor
Alex	Blair	Christina	Elijah
Alexandra	Bobby	Christine	Elizabeth
Alfred	Bradley	Christopher	Emily
Ali	Brandon	Claire	Emma
Alicia	Brant	Cody	Eric
Alison	Brendon	Colleen	Erica
Alix	Brian	Conner	Erin
Alyse	Brianna	Corby	Evan
Alyssa	Brianne	Cory	Everett
Amanda	Brittany	Courtney	Francesca
Amber	Brittny	Crystal	Frank
Amy	Brock	Dan	Gabriella
Andrea	Bruce	Danae	Gary
Andrew	Bryce	Dania	Gene
Anita	C.J.	Danielle	Gianna
Anna	Cameron	Danna	Gina
Anne	Cami	Darla	Grace
Annette	Capri	David	Hannah
Ashlee	Cara	Dean	Haley
Ashley	Carly	Derek	Hilary
Audra	Caroline	Devin	Ian

Isaac	Kaitlin	Kyleigh	Meghan
J.R.	Kaitlyn	Kylie	Melanie
Jackie	Kanani	Kyoko	Melissa
Jacob	Karani	Larry	Michael
Jacquelyn	Karen	Latoya	Michelle
Jake	Kasey	Laura	Mitchell
James	Katelyn	Lauren	Modesty
Jamie	Katerina	Lea	Momiqua
Jasmine	Katey	Leanne	Monique
Jason	Katherine	Lelia	Morgan
Jay	Kathy	Lindsay	Nat
Jeffery	Katie	Lisa	Natalie
Jenna	Katrina	Lola	Neil
Jennifer	Katy	Lori	Nicholas
Jenny	Kawena	Luis	Nick
Jeremiah	Kayla	Lyndsey	Nicole
Jeremy	Kaylee	Lynsey	Nicolus
Jerrod	Keith	Mackenzie	Nikki
Jess	Kelly	Maggie	Olivia
Jesse	Kelsey	Malia	P.J.
Jessica	Kendra	Mandy	Paige
Jimmy	Kenny	Manny	Patrick
Jocelyn	Kevin	Marco	Peter
John	Kevin	Maria	Phillip
Johnathan	Kiersten	Marissa	Rachel
Jonathan	Kimberly	Mark	Randi
Jordan	Knick	Maryanne	Randy
Joseph	Kolby	Mathew	Renee
Josh	Kris	Matt	Rina
Joshua	Krista	Matthew	Robert
Joslyn	Kristi	Maya	Rogelio
Juanita	Kristin	Meagan	Ronnie
Julie	Kristina	Meg	Rory
Justin	Kyle	Megan	Rosie

Russell	Shayle	Taylor	Ty
Ryan	Shelby	Thomas	Tyler
Sam	Sierra	Tiffany	Valarie
Samatha	Stephanie	Timmy	Valeria
Sarah	Stephen	Timothy	Vanessa
Scott	Steve	Tom	Vanessa Anne
Sean	Steven	Tonya	Veronica
Segvoia	Suzanne	Tracey	Victoria
Shannon	Talia	Travis	Vincent
Sharon	Tami	Trista	Vivien Marie
Shastine	Tanya	Troy	Zachary
Shawnee			